Bath Time

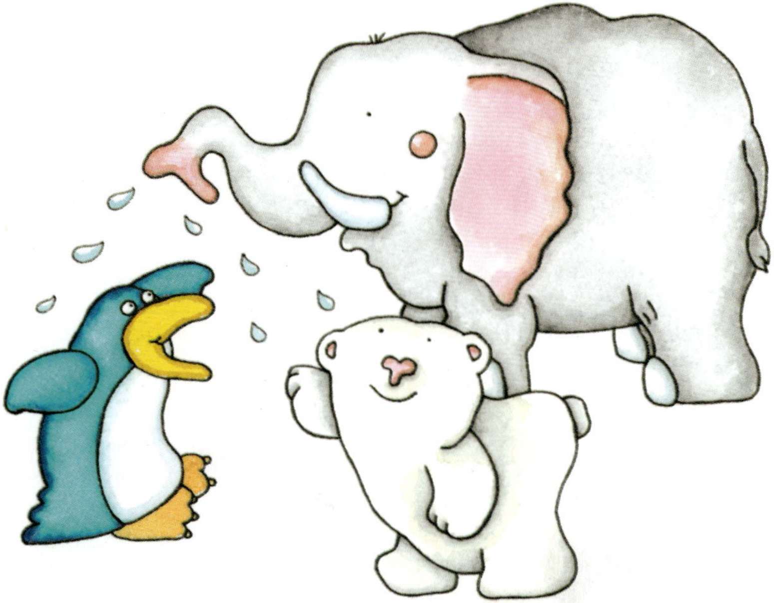

Pippa Goodhart

Illustrated by Charlie Anne Turner

Oxford

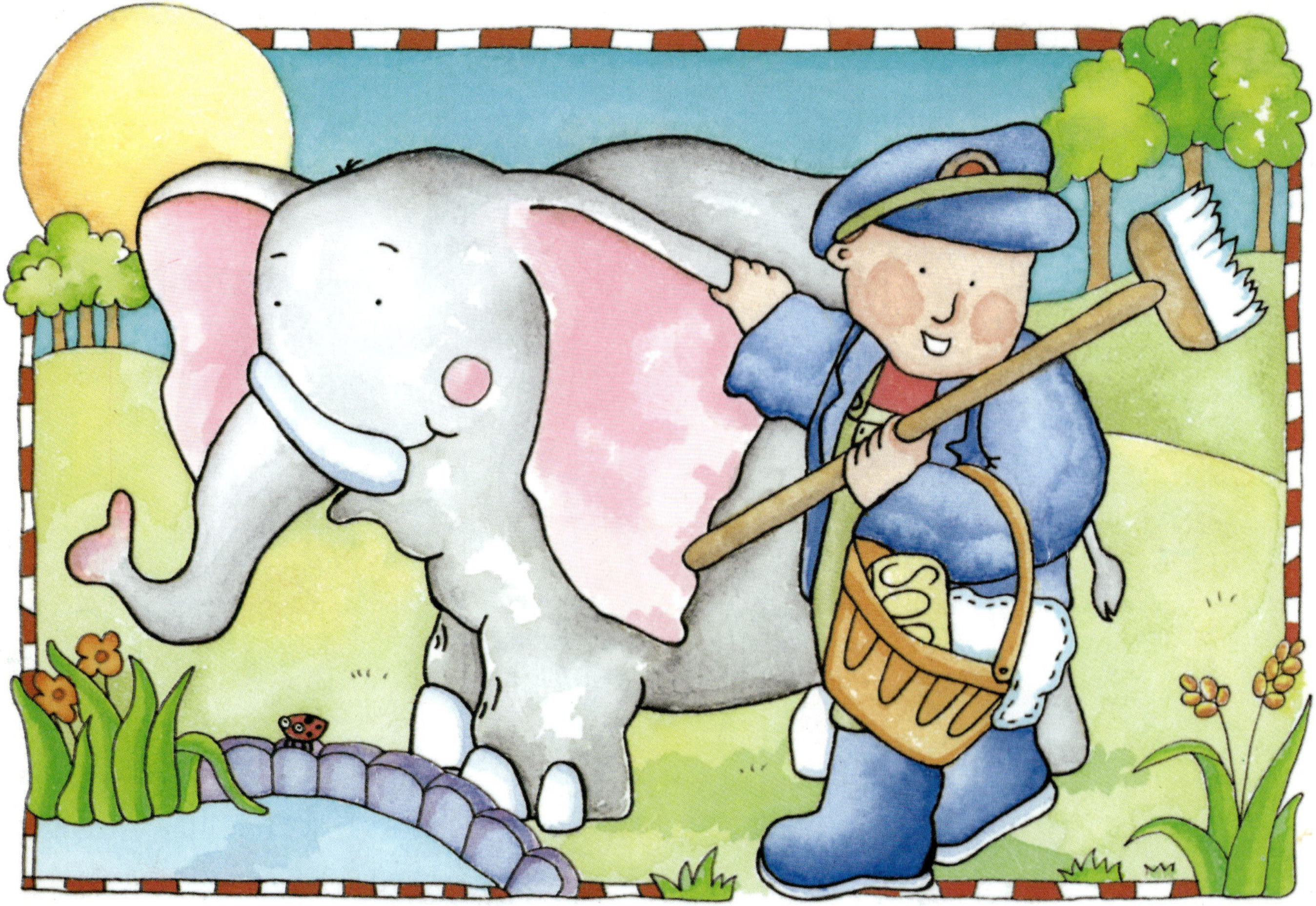

Bath time, elephant.

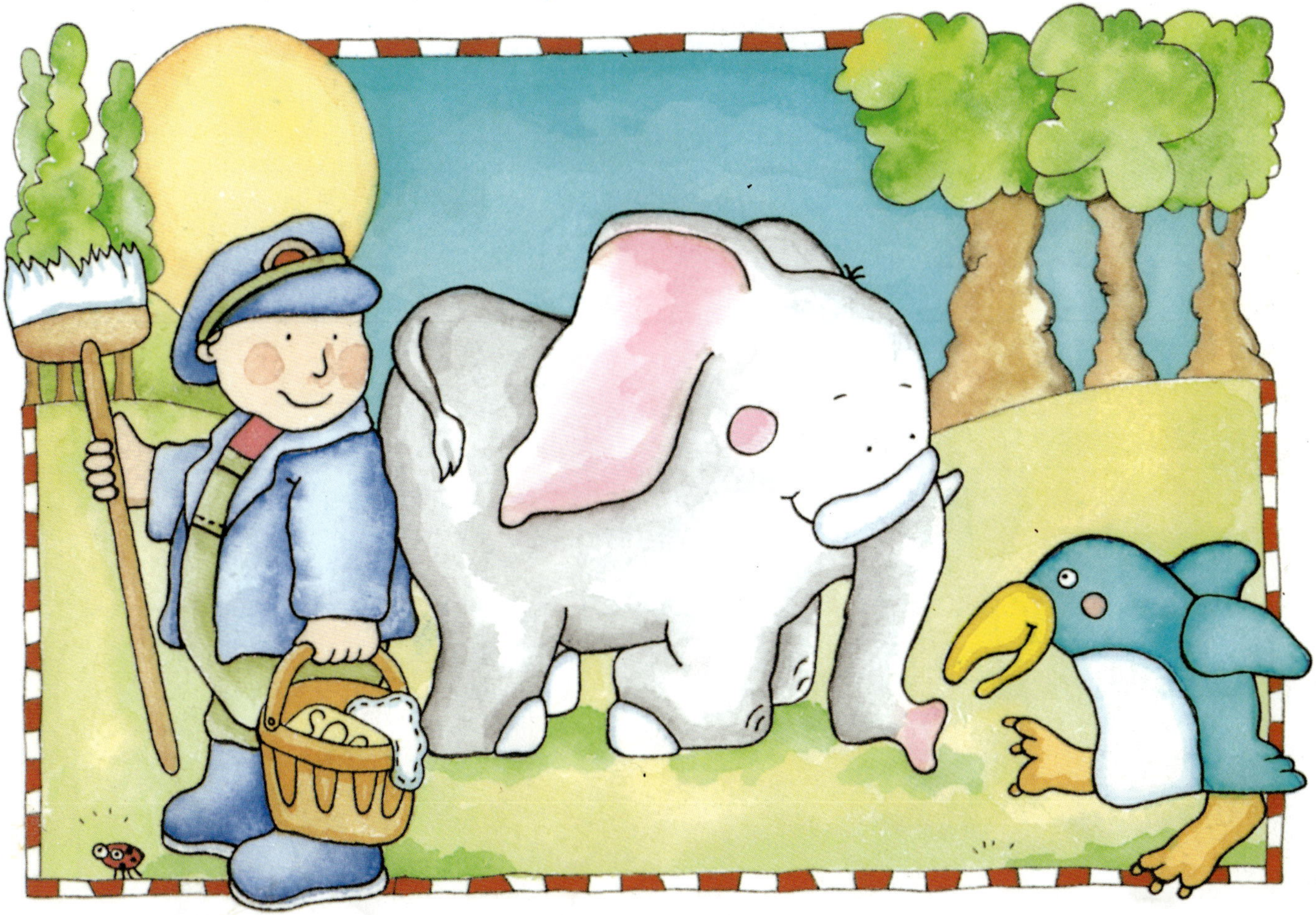

Bath time, penguin.

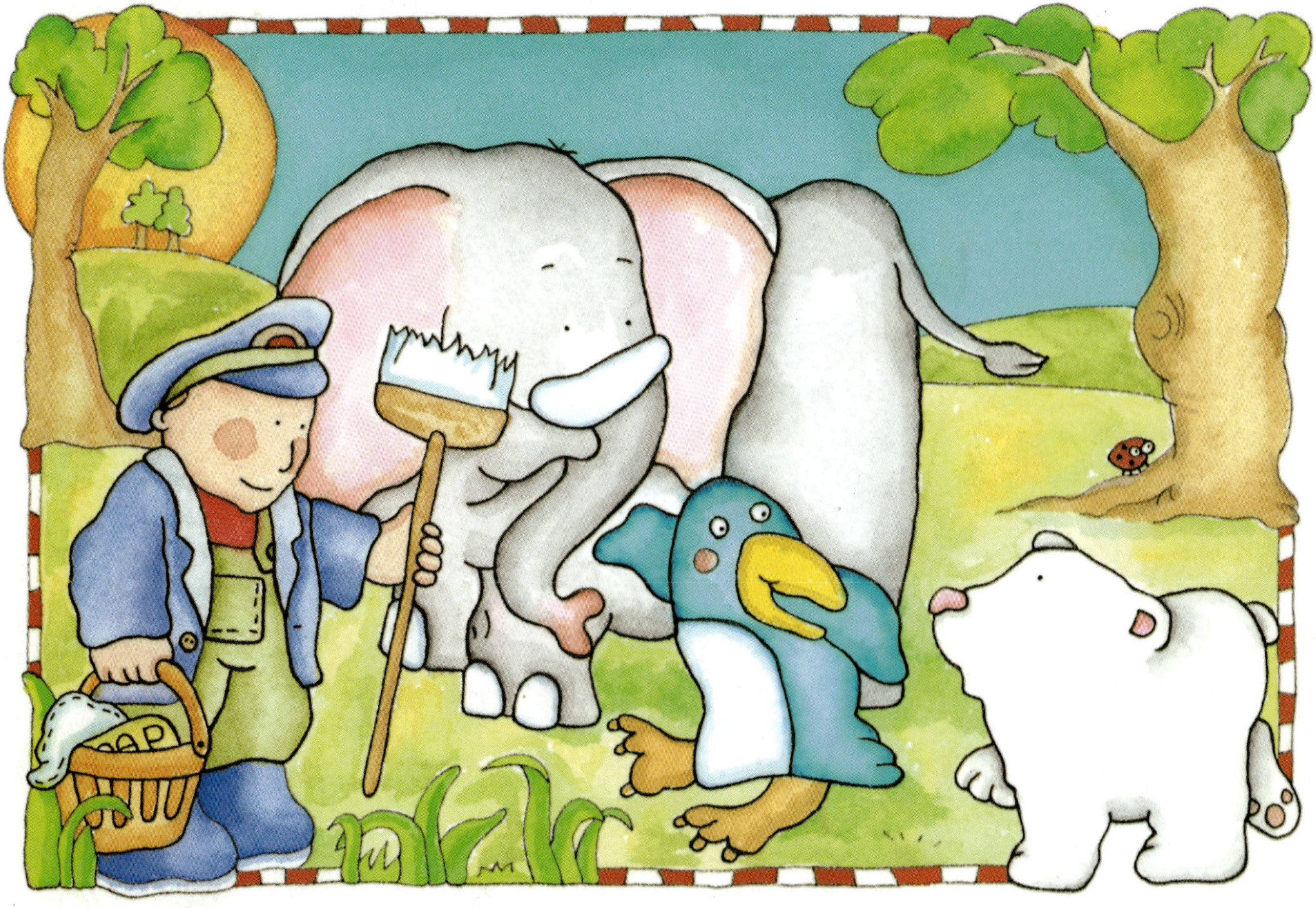

Bath time, bear.

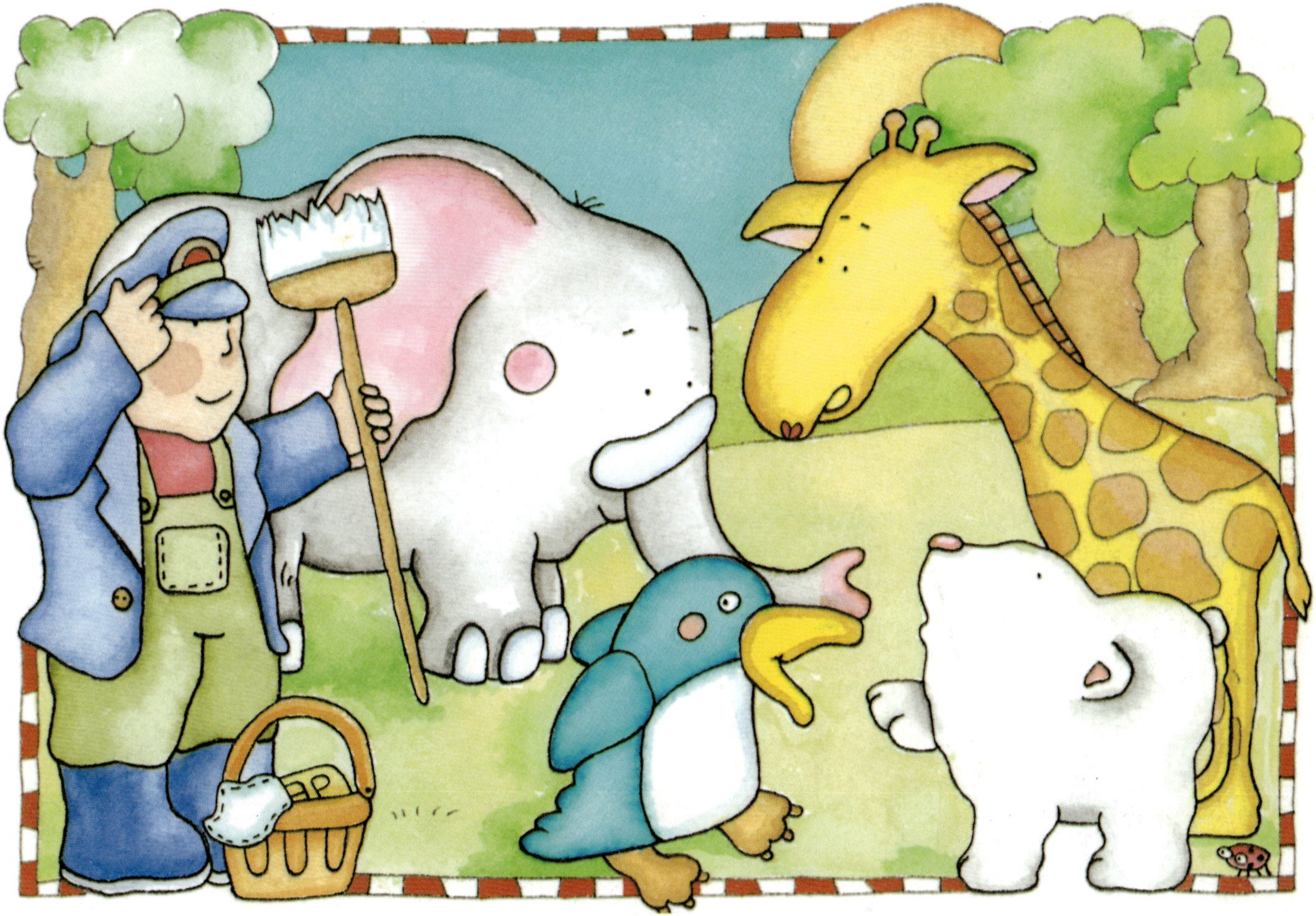

Bath time, giraffe.

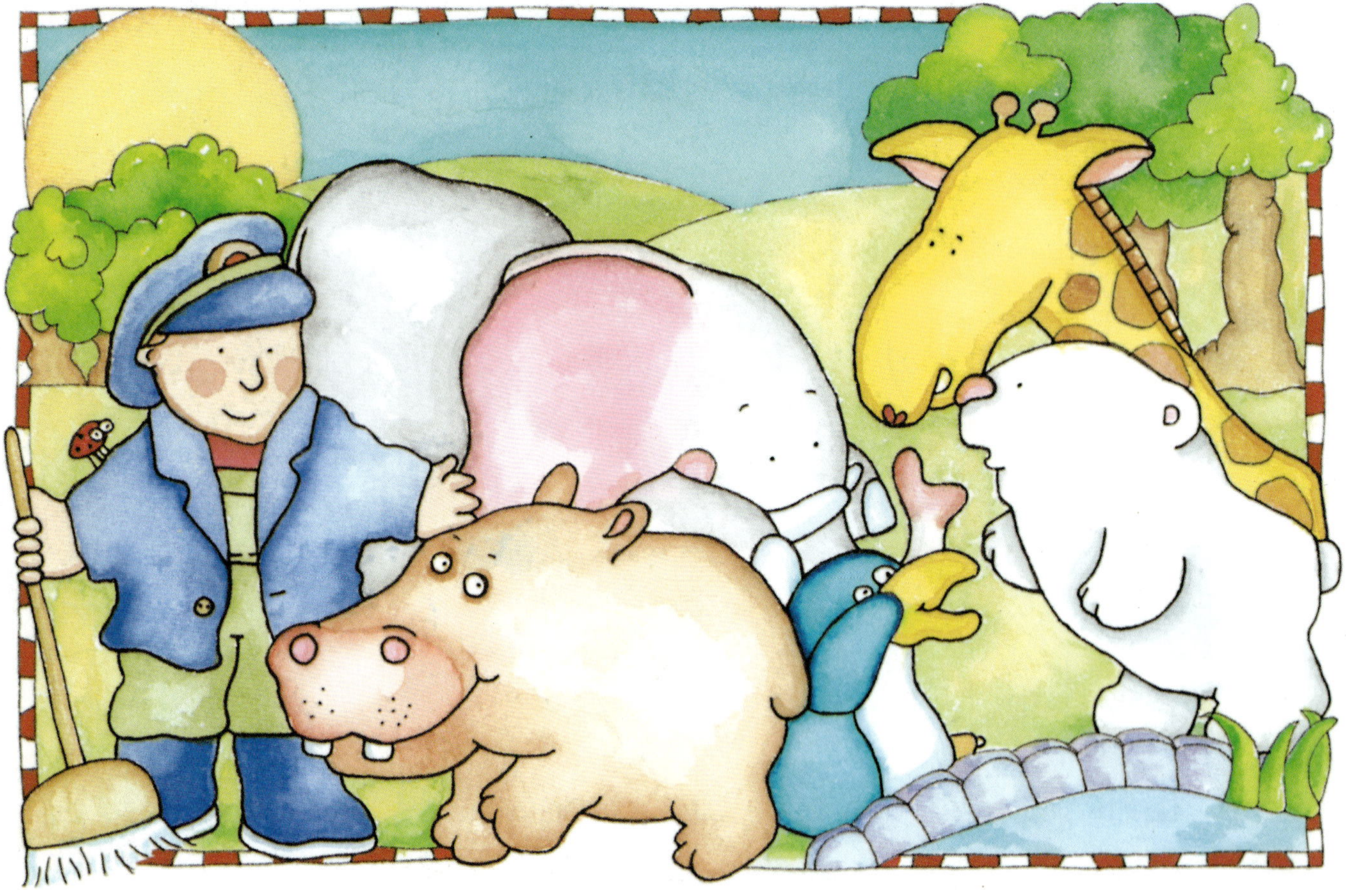

Bath time, hippo.

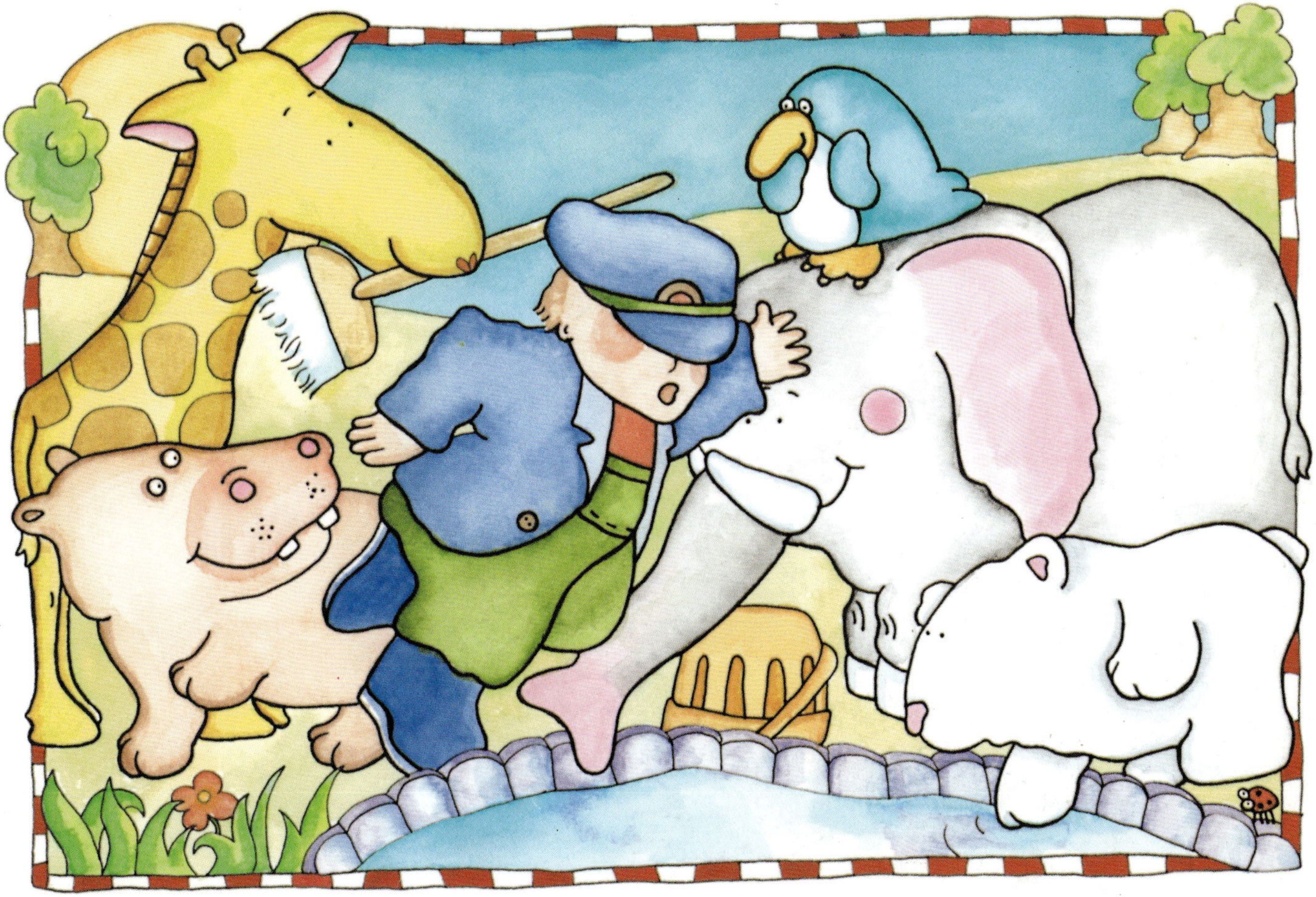

Whoops!

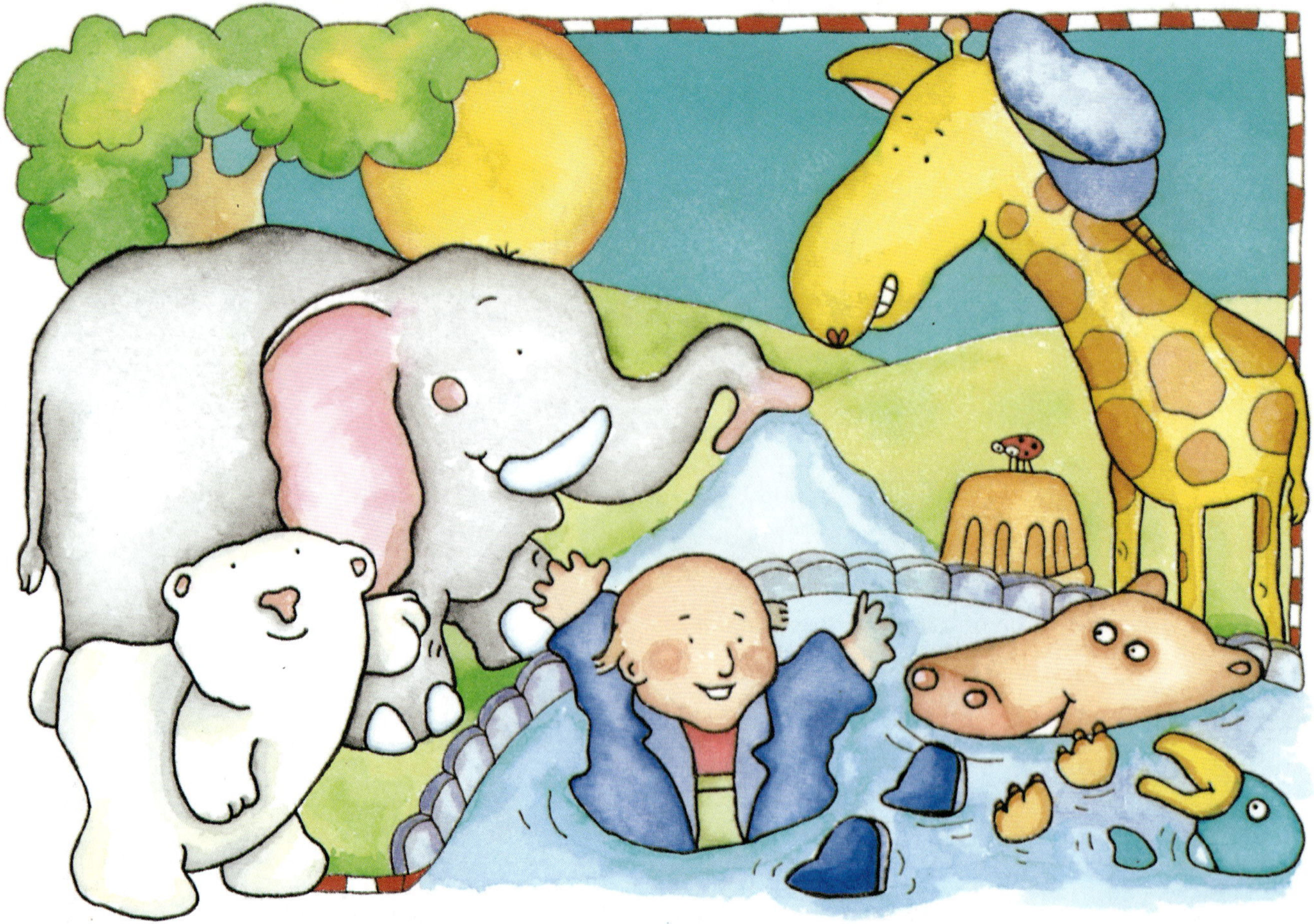

Bath time, Fred!